Ana

Analemma

Scott Andrew James

Big Sun Publishing
10900 Research Blvd Ste 160C PMB 3032 Austin, TX 78759

www.scottandrewjames.com

ISBN: 978-0-9858434-9-6

Book design by Scott Andrew James & Sheila Parr
Cover art adapted from original image by naphoart naphoart

For press or volume book sales, contact Big Sun Publishing

For Liya. And for Kaili.
For saving my life, again and again.
For giving me life, over and over,
From the depths of my heart, forever and ever.
Ah, so.

1

These days we can see our breath.

Orion makes his slow, deliberate pursuit across the sky,
forever hunting, forever shining.

It is in these uncertain mornings that we find the
brightest of suns.

I am reminded that harvest comes from habits.

...

Kaili makes her list in the kitchen,
marking pages with magenta post-it notes.

She is learning how a heart works.
What to keep, what to give away.

...

The world wants me to want things right now,
but I don't. Not today.

...

In the morning I am all wings,
my heart aching to fly
and my eyes awash in sunshine.

By nightfall I need a shovel just to stand.

But no matter.

I know the stars will send their twinkles down
like energy cables,

and I know how to listen through the dark,
where all the courage comes alive.

I will be fueled up by morning.

...

2

It is hard to hold on
to the beauty of the world
as it passes,
so I give it away.

I try to find the wind
a place on paper,
let the light rest
for a moment in words,

Invite the beauty of the world
to land on my hand,
then release it,

giving it, like thanks,
to the world again.

A bird finding a wire,
Then remembering her wings.

...

Maybe this is the way
the heart breathes.
In and out.
Back and forth.

An invitation
to choose to offer everything,
making room somehow to hold it all again
when it is new
and returning.

...

3

I am always standing
in front of infinite doors,

Surrounded by choices
that are not freedom.

Choosing a door.
Walking through it.
Not looking back.

That is freedom.
That is the new world
where the power breathes.

I live inside those decisions like fresh air
in a world made of wings.

...

4

We've been painting again,
out on the back porch.

Kaili mixes colors, makes playful strokes.
She adds sand from the sandbox,
dirt, coffee, tea, and all kinds of stuff.
Boogers even.

She walks away and leaves everything outside.
I've taken to leaving it all out there.
As if the paintings are not finished
until they go through the rain and wind and sun.

They are the most beautiful things
I think I've ever seen.

This is what spring looks like for me.

Trust the process, not the plan.

Sometimes it is time
to leave myself out in the rain and the sun and get
windswept. Let the colors blend and return to their
rainbow ways, feel what it feels like when the rains have
come and gone and come again. Let the new summer
sun remind me how everything looks in the light.

...

5

Today,
I want simple.

Today,
I want a single word
that means
everything.

Today,
I want the quiet
that follows
to be a blanket.

A favorite chair
that asks no questions,

A breath that takes
the cruddy stuff out,

and leaves me
with still waters
under wind,

quiet reasons,
strong within.

This is how
my winter will begin.

What weather without
will I invite in?

6

I am not
What my head
Is afraid of,

Love is what
My heart
Is made of.

Thank you, fear,
For pointing me
Right at what
I needed to see.

7

The things I fear
are a magical garden.

The fires I shrink from
are also the sun.

Ye, though I walk in the valley
of the shadow of death,
I also feel
the cool summer breeze.

...

Which dream am I having?
What will I invite into my eyes?
What words live in my mind?

...

I turn
in the direction
of my instincts.

The real work is calling.

Like an apple bobbing in a river in the rain in my heart,
the future is waiting for me to ask it to dance,
whatever I mean & whichever I believe.

...

Tell someone you love what you want to be in 3 years,
instead of rehashing the last ten.

Tell someone you love them instead of evaluating their
decisions.

Tell someone what you are afraid of and ask them how
they see you.

...

The things I fear
are magical gardens.

My truth has little to do with the world,
and everything to do with myself.

...

8

While I wait,
wanting things
in the way of other things
to go away,

I wonder if wanting
is in the way
of the way I need
to go.

I hold my hopeful breath,
because I don't know.

...

I will sit
and breathe
for a bit,

Listen
to my heart
go thumpa
thumpa
thumpa
and..

...

I will thank
all the things
that have come before now
that have turned into now
that have formed into
the informed now.

...

I will ask myself
(out loud if I can)
to be the soft thrust
that punches
through the fog,

To be one who remembers.
To use my hands to create.
To let each breath sing.

...

I will ask a question
That is a quest:

WHAT IS POSSIBLE
WHEN I AM PART OF WHAT'S NEXT?

9

Every morning
we go underwater.

We swim
with the whales
and the dolphins.

...

She says,

If humans were dolphins,
would we still think
they are this beautiful?

I say,

I think dolphins know
how beautiful the other dolphins are,
the way I know
how beautiful you are.

...

We watch the divers
twist and spin,
their bodies
a breath away
from the whale's mouth.

And fear is a third thing floating between them.
Or maybe it's just called awe.

I didn't know
how it could be
so peaceful
down there.

...

We all sit together and watch.
Together.

We are watching the depths.
The quiet dangers.
The unspeakable beauty.

...

Somehow we decide
every morning
to do it again.

I think it has to be like this.

...

We must choose
every morning
to breathe
deep underneath
the things we are afraid of.

That
is where
the beauty
is waiting to swim with us.

10

Yes, I will make
of each day
an altar with my words,

Speak my life into being,
From this cruddy/muddy muck,

Up through these guttural utterances
& into the light

Where I have no right to shine
But I will shine anyway.

My blood is wine.
My body is a poem.

I am getting better
With age, if only

I can listen
To the wind in my open heart.

...

11

The morning light
It said to me,
Life is simple
If you let it be.

...

12

These times are slushy.

Groundless, like tectonic plates under our feet, moving again before they sit still.

I want to remind you, as I remind myself and the people I love in my house every day, that you are in control of you.

You are in control of how you react and how you show up.

You are in control of how you breathe and the words that come out of your mouth.

I tell myself this as I pause.
I tell myself this as I breathe deep.
I tell myself this as I choose love.

...

The world is the world.
Your heart is YOURS.

Be good to yourself.
Be good to each other.

...

We are not at war.
We are trying to love ourselves and each other.
And it is hard.
Oh, God, is it hard.

...

TODAY,
I AM SO ALIVE,
EVEN TIME
IS ON MY SIDE.

...

13

Kaili wakes early again.

Something rumbling in a dream
that wakes before the light.

Is something wrong, my love?
I don't know.

We go to watch the whales together.

...

This documentary
feels like fiction.

Why do the beautiful things
seem so far away?

...

My heart wants to be a polar bear,
My soul a seal,

And narwhals whisper
that magic is real.

...

I don't want to be lost
In the ocean,
I want to be the ocean.

...

I don't want to be the ocean.
I am the ocean.
We are the ocean.
...

We are the giant, undulating depths
That rage and fall
And fold over back on ourselves.

We are the massive deep
That reminds us of ourselves
When we sleep.

We are the source of life,
Asking for nothing
But forgiveness and progress.

We are the forgiveness
That does not come
Until everything else
Is done.

...

On the dark stairs,
her fingers hold my hand.

It is quiet enough
not to think,

So I don't.

...

We are pitter patter feet
Before the dawn.

Is something wrong?
Yes, many things are wrong.

And also,
There is love.

...

Love,
Like an ocean
that has no shore,

Love,
like a voyage
that always has more.

14

Summer lingers,
the heat staying stuck inside us.

Autumn clears its throat,
and sets us free.

We welcome the rhythms of returning,
of school, of learning, of working.
It is not normal but it is closer.
We are growing and changing.

We are learning new habits
for this new world.

We are messy
on our way to our best.

...

I hear stories now.
This year has made us stare
at the hollow places inside ourselves.
At how we fill those hollow places.

. . .

What is in my heart
will get into my life.
The dreaming, the fearing,
I hold the light.

15

It rains today as if it will rain
forever.

We reach for something, some kind
of umbrella.

But it is not being dry
that will keep us alive,

It is covering each other, soaking wet
but together.

...

We are not the sadness.

We are human beings with hearts
Whose highest power is to love.

...

16

I am not
The words I speak,
I am the mystery
From which they leap.

....

17

I believe
that creativity
is a divine wind
blowing all around me,
all the time.

It is up to me
to clear out my heart,
breathe deep,
and let the wind in.

...

What comes through
is not mine,
but I do
give it life.

My job is to direct the wind.
To point the breeze.
To interpret the many faces of the air.

...

In the end,
this body will return to dust
and be blown about on distant roads.

For now, this body holds a heart,
beating with the power of the sun rising & setting,
relentless like waves finding & releasing the beach,
pumping like gears greased with love greater than fear.

...

18

This heart is a way of being.

I will call to the wind
and be a conduit.

Let it through
and be free to do
what it will.

I will show up, ready to serve.
I will show up and say Yes.
I will show up, and let the wind in.

...

What is the difference,
Between wishing and wanting?
Between prayer and intention?
Between asking and knowing?
Between becoming and being?

...

It is ok to be powerful.
In fact, it is necessary.

...

The world does not need us to use
our inside voices.

The world needs my question mark
to become a lightning bolt,
descending from the sky
amidst the storm to say

This. Now. Me. Us. Here.

...

Moonlight
is reflected sunlight --
the same and yet different.

There is no right way
to use my light --
but I do need to shine.

...

The difference?

Me.

...

Between
wishing and wanting,
prayer and intention,
asking and knowing,
becoming and being

Is me.

...

Me and my heart
are the difference.

...

19

I wake up,
and wish there was
something beautiful in my heart,
but instead it's a sore muscle,

...

Downstairs,
we work the knot,
pressing against
what we cannot see.

Something is wrong,
but we're not sure what.

...

The old books
did not prepare us for this.

The old stories
do not know what to do.

...

I want there to be an answer,
but there is only
the will to keep going.

...

Today,

Instead of running through time,
I will breathe.

Instead of needing to be right,
I will just be.

I will ask the sun
to wash me with heat

and ask the rain
for a drink.

Instead of wondering,
I will walk in the woods,

Pressing against
what I cannot see
with the simple truths
that I can still do.

Something will be the right answer,
even if I am not sure what.

...

Today,
my heart still beats
like a beautiful, magnificent secret,

and that
is where I will begin.

...

20

Every day I say
It is not my problem,
But every day
It is deeply my problem,

Heaving and bleating
On the helpless sand.

I am sure it cannot get worse
And then it gets worse.

I am sure it is somewhere else
And then it is inside me.

I am sure I can forget
And then it is coming sideways out of my mouth.

...

I am checking things off the infinite list.
I am blinking into the sun.
I am loving as my heart breaks.
I am in the thick of it when I thought I was done.

I am a deep breath in heavy traffic.
I somehow receive the gifts I give.
The answer is mine when I don't think I have it.
I am screaming until I am singing.

...

There's a way.
There's a way.
There's a way.
There's a way.
There's a way.

...

There is a way forward.
And I know it must go through me.

...

IT'S A GIFT, NOT A TEST

21

I can tell you about chaos,

how the wind
and the rain
are everywhere and everything,

even on
a sunny day.

...

I can tell you about loss,
how everything
slows down,
as if time
forgets
how to move.

...

I can even tell you about fear,

how I am afraid
of so many things
that I do not look at
and will not name,

how the fear
feels like
it is outside of me,
but it is not.

...

I can tell you
about picking
at the paint,

waiting
to change,
Later.

...

But instead,

I will tell you
that today

is a day to say
I love you.

...

Wherever you are
and whatever you are doing,
the world needs your voice.

There is someone
who you are not telling
who you could be telling.

And that
will change
the world.

Your world.

...

There is a space
that will sing
when you say it,

And that space
is the space
where all the stories live.

...

Go say it.
And change

22

If there were an umbrella
wide enough to keep everything we are afraid of
from falling like angry rain into my life,

I would use it.

...

I'm glad
there's not.

Through
is the better way
to get through.

23

The wind
is a heartbeat
that knows the way.

Listen,
and listen,
and listen again.

...

In that place where new things
rise up like morning mist,
I am singing.

I am
a prayer
finding its voice.

...

The fresh air
is always
"over there."

I will breathe it,
and I will be somehow different
and more myself.

...

These reasons
I plant like a garden,
will grow into everything I need,

as surely
as I hold them now,
these quiet, magnificent seeds.

...

I will give away
What I want to stay.

...

To grow
is to stretch
limbs
past where things are certain.

If I knew the road
it would just be a room
in my house.

...

I will keep going
until what I find
is more true
than what I leave behind.

I AM NOT A MISTAKE.
I AM MADE BY THE CHOICES I MAKE.
AND I AM WORTH THE WAIT.

Find the wind
and keep going.

24

The world will teach me
one thing,
and then remind me
I know nothing.

This, I am convinced,
is what it means to learn.

To find repeatedly,
like an ocean's waves,

that everything I discover
turns out to make
more space.

No wonder
the universe is expanding!

...

25

It is the waves
that make sense,
not the standing
in the sand.

...

I remember
the feel of wind
behind my wishing.

I know it is not the remembering
that pulls the sun up
from that blind horizon —

It is the wish,
simple and certain
from my lips
that makes room
for the light,

offering up
the fresh depths
of my breath.

I AM WHAT GROWS INSIDE
THE SPACE I MAKE
WHEN I LET GO.

...

26

When I look in the mirror
There is no face,
Just a road.

...

I ask the hard questions
because that is where
the future lives.

I want to change the world,
but I can barely get my daughter
to eat breakfast.

All I know
is that
I am not finished.

...

The way through myself
is the way to myself.

This new self
will be a true self.

I AM NOT FINISHED.

...

27

I will not tell you the truth
That was told to me,
I will tell you the truth
That I find.

...

We must remember in new ways.
We must discuss what we cannot find words for.
We must invite what is uncomfortable
To break bread with our beliefs.

...

Watch as the paint curls from the walls we've built
around ourselves,

Remember when we thought the walls were something
more than imagining, when they were always just air?

...

Believe in what remains.
Like a still, simple flame.
Right there, calm
In the middle of the wind.

...

So many times what we know
Is in the way of where we need to go.

28

When the dreams come,
early morning
and reckless,

they are a breeze
moving leaves
across my porch.

...

The universe
clears its throat,

and I am flung ashore
on some familiar, strange beach.

...

It is true that the past is still with us,
but it is more true that it is gone,

Or, always leaving.
Like a faucet dripping,
all night.

...

We must answer the questions
that these silences bring up,

We must piece ourselves back together
with the imperfect tools
already in our hands.

...

No one is coming to save us.

They have already come
and they are still here.

I am still here.

...

I will believe in what is coming
more than what has come before,

I will believe I am becoming,
becoming something more.

I will understand I am a portal,
not just a swinging door.

...

I will say Yes
again and again
until I am singing
with a defiant insistence
that sounds like nothing else
so much as
myself.

I WILL BELIEVE.
THIS IS HOW
MY SOUL WILL BREATHE.

29

Tomorrow is not a risk,
it is a wish.

...

The world is doing
whatever the world is doing,
(or not doing),

and so are you
(or not).

...

The future is not fragile.

It is waiting for fingers
and kneading and mashing,

Ready for the rigors
of vigorous asking.

...

Turn the walls of the room
into the walls of a tunnel.

And keep going.

...

Sometimes the light
is in front of me,

And sometimes the light
is inside me.

But every time
the light is shining.

...

I AM NOT MY FEARS.

I AM WHATEVER PROMISES
I HOLD DEAR.

...

Keep going, wherever the light is.

It is true that I am waiting,
and it is true that I hate waiting.

It is true that some days
I wake up hollowed out,
still filled with fast-forward dreams
that don't let me rest.

It is true that the wilderness of my neighborhood,
is heavy with sameness.

...

But I cannot tell you about these things
without also telling you
about the yellow flowers.

...

They are everywhere,
like indiscriminate sunshine
thrown by a magic hand.

They grow on the hills
where my daughter and I run.

Two years old and luminous,
she picks them up like infinite gifts,

lifting them from the earth
with a playful certainty
I want to put in a bottle
for myself.

Her laughter is so pure
it feels like it is against the rules.
But it is not.

The yellow flowers say:
Everything you need to love
still works.

31

At the bottom of the bottom
There is a heart that has its own heart.

It will save us
But we will not know how.

We will try to ask its name
but it will not tell,

It will simply hold up a mirror
like a sword waiting underwater
to remind us who we are.

...

32

I know that I am not alone,
but I constantly forget it.

I catch myself
thinking to myself
that I want to stop thinking!

What else makes sense but to laugh?

These ruthless mornings
stretch out like noise bouncing off too many walls.

Where will I go when
it is time for going again?

Why am I no different
when it is already next time?

When can I hug
thinking of nothing but love?

...

33

Today,
I will not think too hard.

Today,
I will be grateful for the not knowing.

Today,
I will make the sound that my heart is making,

The rhythm that sounds like the beginning
that comes up from the depths
as if it were brand new
every time:

Thank you.

Thank you.

Thank you.

It is only together
that we can be ourselves.

...

34

This is the secret.
You are the secret.

And we are holding these secrets
like promises in imaginary jars.

It is time to turn the lid,
to break the glass,
and to use the wings
we have been building.

...

I believe.

Not because I need to,
but because this is how
the breath works best.

...

FORGIVE THE MISTAKE,
INVENT THE FUTURE.

This is the song
The shadows are singing.

...

35

You will not know it is happening
until it is happening.

You will simply feel
your heart loosening,

like a screw you have been working on
almost too long
but not long enough to give up
and then...

Pop.

...

But what happened is still happening,
and what happened was you.

And what happened is still inside you,
like tiny sailboats of longing somewhere deep in the
blood.

And what will happen next is you, too.

...

What will happen
is the sun will come out again,

and when it does
we will remember how to shine.

We will take our shadows back outside
and shake them off like ghost dogs,
like wet rugs on the back porches of memory.

And we will see what is left,
And we will see what is missing,

And we will do what needs to be done.

...

36

Look for the question
and the answer appears.

Like yawning arms
first thing in the morning,

the thing we need
wants to come out,

if we can find the strength
to get out of the way.

...

37

I like laughter
because it doesn't need a reason.

I like how it doesn't change,
but is always different.

And I like how it finds a way
to happen anyway,

whatever happens
to be in the way.

I want that when it counts.

...

38

The truth I want
is not about answers.

It is about how we ask,
and what we ask,
and where we let our wonder go.

...

This is where
the yawning has room to stretch out
and shake cobwebs from corners,

Where truth can make
whatever noise it makes,

Where questions
can be lessons.

We stand in awe.
We take a breath.
We take a step.
Everything we need is in everything we get.

FIND A WAY TO PLAY.

39

We are in the world
in a new way now,

even if that world
is not the world
we knew.

...

At night we do not sleep much.

We say we think maybe it's bad dreams but
it's hard to know the difference.

...

Everything hurts,
in the familiar ways
and in some new ones.

But it will not crush my heart
like a raspberry.

...

This morning
we will be awake
in new ways.

...

We will punch the clocks
in our hearts,

And we will make room
to do the work.

We will hold on
to the sunlight climbing through the window,

and hold space
for the laughter exploring the room.

We will hold each other
in whatever ways we can.

This is the way
we will continue to stand.

...

I WANT SOMETHING MORE.
NOT JUST OVER,
BUT BETTER THAN BEFORE.

IT'S NOT EITHER/OR.

I AM WAVES NOW,
FINDING THE SHORE.

40

These days,
we are seldom with each other
or with ourselves.

This is the way
when the sunshine curls up like a question mark.

...

We are building the future one day at a time,
But we do not know when that future will be.

We stack bricks into a wall standing between now and
forever,
We sing songs across time zones that are out of sync
with our mouths moving,
We go to sleep as if tomorrow will be different,
will be more,
will be something
we have not seen before.

...

My brother calls and we talk
late into the night.

We are asking for small favors that feel like lifelines.
We are talking and it feels like crying.
We are crying and it feels like talking.
We are lifelines crying out for small favors.

...

When we hang up,
the world is still blurry through midnight's wet window.

But tomorrow is not a hologram.

Tomorrow is a dream
that will wake up as strong as I am.

...

THE THING IS...

IT WILL TAKE
EVERYTHING FROM EACH OF US
TO BECOME
One,

AND WHAT
I GIVE AWAY
IS SOMEHOW
WHAT I WILL BECOME.

41

Outside,
the sky throws angry water
at windows.

We open a door to listen.
We watch with our ears.

A smile is a smile,
whatever the weather.

...

She drinks milk,
I drink coffee.

Together, we feel
the thunder rumble.

Together, we feel
the ancient calm of the storm.

...

It teaches us how to stand still.

It reminds us how to create
even as we flush out the nasty.

It shows us how to love
when our blood wants to run.

...

The sun breaks through,

Our feet move out the door,
into the light where the ripples are everywhere!

And we are splashing in the puddles,
And we are laughter in the shimmers
And we are saying to the light,

Yes, I understand.

...

THE PURSUIT
IS THE WISDOM,
NOT THE SITTING
WITH THE KNOWING.

I DO NOT NEED
TO BE PERFECT,
I JUST NEED
TO KEEP GOING.

I NEED
TO KEEP DANCING
ANYWAY.

...

42

It does not get easier,
but somehow it gets better.

I tell myself a story
that will become my story.

This is how the future works.

...

Starts and stops.
Hopes and dreams.
Realities and mistakes.

...

I collect water leftover in a glass,
I smooth the crooked sheet of paper,
and I rescue the paints from the sudden spring sun.

I make something new.

Meanwhile, their magnificent voices come alive in the
living room.
They are discovering a puzzle for the hundredth time,
They are finding a new reason to laugh.

I do not need to have it figured out.

I only need
to keep going
and to love.

...

I BELIEVE
IN MAKING A HOME
FOR THAT WHICH
DOES NOT HAVE
A HOME YET,

THIS IS HOW
THE FUTURE WORKS.

THIS IS HOW
I BECOME
WHAT'S NEXT.

43

I remember what it is
to shake hands with a stranger,
to say without saying,
"I am safe, and so are you,"

I remember what it is
to hug without question,
to hold on a bit longer
just because.

I remember
what it is like
to be far, far apart
and also so invisibly together.

I remember,
and I will remember.

And from there, I will create.

...

HERE IS WHERE
THE BEGINNING BEGINS,

WHERE THE HEART PUMPS THE BLOOD
OUT INTO OUR LIMBS.

44

So I ask myself,

What do I believe about myself?
Why do I believe it?
How old is that belief and is it still serving me?

Is it a gift I want to give to my future?
How will I breathe life into everything I do today?
How do I make each thing I do today great?

...

And then I stop.

And I move.

And it gets easier.

And I become.

...

I LET GO OF THE QUESTIONS
LIKE BIRDS INTO THE SKY,

I SAY YES TO THE LESSONS
WITH NO WORDS AND NO WHY.

45

It is not easy to stay light
when the world is heavy.

But it is possible.
And it is important.
And it is healing.

Light is contagious.
And we need it to shine.

...

FEAR IS A FALSE PROPHET
FEEDING ME THE CURSE
OF TINY THINKING.

INSTEAD,
I WILL NOURISH MY BODY
WITH THE GIANT SONG OF THE TRUTH

AND I WILL HOLD ON WITH MY HEART
TO WHAT IS ASKING FOR LOVE,
AND IN THE WIND,
I WILL STAND FIRM AND BEGIN.

46

The world is so heavy
with concern, with worry, with blockades.

The darkness waits for me at night,
filled with trojan horses galloping
on splintered lullabyes.

They sing to me out of tune.
And I listen.

I want to be still,
to hold each worry lightly,
like a paper lantern,
to sing powerful, soothing songs to their darkness.

Then fall asleep together into a deep rest
where we can spread everything out on a table,
sort it into piles,
and put it in its place again.

...

We are so busy being heavy,
trying hard
to hold each other up.

Breathe a bit
And remember how
We fit together.

...

THE HEART
IS A CAVE
HOLDING DARKNESS
AND LIGHT,

I AM THE HERO
AND THE DRAGON,
AND THE QUEST
IS MY LIFE.

47

Once, I took a trip
with my bag packed
only half full.

Instead of stuff stuffed to the zippers --
I had room.

Empty space.

It was great.

...

I glided through security.
I was light on my feet.
I knew where everything was and how to find it.

When I found a shirt I liked on the boardwalk,
I had room to bring it home.

...

I want my brain to feel like that.

Not too full to learn something new,
Space to see the sunlight.

Enough air
to lift the wings up
when the runway says let's go.

A QUESTION
IS DIRECTION
WHEN I HAVE ROOM
TO FIND IT,

THE ANSWER
IS A DANCER –
WITH THE WIND
BEHIND IT.

48

Whatever my heart
is doing today,

cartwheels or
cannonballs,

there is room in the universe
for me.

...

The void will say Yes
when I stretch into it.

And nothing
will ever be the same.

...

WE DON'T NEED ANSWERS,
WE NEED A PURPOSE

THAT GETS US
TO THE PEOPLE

THAT GETS US
TO THE POWER.

49

I am always standing
in front of infinite doors,

but that
is not freedom.

Choosing a door
and walking through.

That is the freedom.
That is the thing.
That is the new world where power breathes.

And I live inside those decisions like fresh air
in a world made of wings.

...

EVEN WHEN
THE ROAD TO TOMORROW
IS PAVED WITH FEAR,
IT LEADS ME EVER FURTHER
INTO THE LIGHT.

AND WE ARE ON IT
TOGETHER.

KEEP GOING.

50

When I am away,
I can recognize my personal geography.

How the decisions I make, make me.

How the weather in my head
does what rain and volcanoes do
to these islands,

How the cycles of my breathing
are waves on the shores of my heart.

...

I will travel
until I do not need the map,

Until what I discover as a mystery
becomes a gift I can offer,

Until the sky of every place
becomes the connected sky of a single place.

I will call it home,
and never stop saying thank you.

...

WHEREVER I VENTURE,
WANDER OR ROAM,
MY HEART IS A COMPASS
THAT KNOWS THE WAY HOME.

51

While I make plans,
my daughter is laughing.

The sound brings me back
to right now, where I have been all along.

...

Who really understands
these invisible things?

Like wind,
or wishes,
or all this breathing in and out?

...

Be patient.
Do good work.
Burn the dreams of the night before
every morning.

Walk into the light empty & open
& ready to carry what is new.

...

BESIDE THE OCEAN,
I REMEMBER THAT THINKING
IS NOT THE WAY,
IT IS IN THE WAY.
SAY THE ETCH-A-SKETCH WAVES.
MMMMMMMMM

52

A storm never tells the whole truth.

From the ground it only shows
the bottom of the weather.

What's inside is anyone's guess.

...

In the rain and shadows,
we must be our own light.

My part of the storm
must be true.

...

THE LIGHTNING
IS NOT THE SKY ATTACKING,

IT IS THE SKY
REMIDING ME
WHAT MY LIGHT
IS CAPABLE OF,

WHATEVER THE WEATHER.

53

Disappointment is a letter from the future.

It reads like the Me
I want to be.

I am grateful for the tension.

...

Now is the right time to ask for help,
to speak the deep truth,

and to live this moment
like the brave decision
I know I need to be.

...

I HEAR MY HEARTBEAT
KNOCKING
FROM DEEP INSIDE.

A NEW SELF
SAYING, LET ME OUT,
I WILL NOT HIDE.

54

I recognize you, fear.

Especially at this time of year.

I know you want me sitting still, spinning in messy spirals. You make so much noise that sometimes I forget That I am telling you what to say.

...

This time,
I will find a secret in the hidden gradients.
I will buzz with the soft electricity of beginnings.
I will radiate with light that does not need words.

And I know you will be there, too.

We will do this anyway. All the way.

...

HELLO, FEAR,
TAKE MY HAND,
LET'S DO THIS
TOGETHER.

I AM NOT POWERFUL WITHOUT,
I AM POWERFUL
WITHIN.

55

The beginning comes before the belief.
That is fine. It will make sense later.

These hands can weave something whole
out of what the mind cannot connect.

Yet.

This is how the world is made. One beginning at a
time. Until everything is beginning. All at once.

Like a symphony singing
as if it were singular.

...

SOMETIMES I FORGET THAT SAYING

"I AM GOOD AT THIS"
COMES AFTER

"I AM DOING THIS"
WHICH COMES AFTER

"I BELIEVE"
WHICH COMES AFTER

"I BEGIN"

ALL OF THESE THINGS
LIVE DOWN UNDER MY SKIN.

56

WHEN I THINK I KNOW
I DO NOT KNOW,

WHEN I ACT,
IT IS SO CLEAR
I COULD BUILD A UNIVERSE
INSIDE IT.

...

IT APPEARS
LIKE SWEAT WHEN
I DANCE WITH THE POSSIBLE,

GLISTENING LIKE
A PROMISE MADE
OF PURE LIGHT.

...

THESE WILD VEINS
TRUST THE RHYTHM
INSIDE THEM.

57

Something about the distance says Yes.
We have what we need for the road we have left.
When we arrive there will be enough time then to rest.
For now we can burn the deep fuel of self.

BELIEVE & THE PATH APPEARS,
TO PAVE THE WAY
RIGHT OVER THE FEAR.

58

You must begin, despite a strong wind.

Every day the unexpected wins out over inertia. A galaxy
is born. A mountain expands by a grain of sand. Our
cells regenerate as we check email and cook
dinner. Love decides that it is time to dance. Again.

You must begin, despite a strong wind.
You are the weather you need to get better.

...

WHEN THE DARKNESS IS HEAVY,
THE IDEA OF LIGHT IS LIGHT.

HOLD IT LIKE A DECISION
BEING BORN
DESPITE A STRONG WIND.

NOW IS MY TIME,
SAYS THE LIGHT.

I WILL BLOW
INTO THE NEW FLAME
IN MY HANDS
LIKE MY LIFE
DEPENDS ON IT,

BECAUSE IT DOES.

59

The incremental is the path to the infinite.

To achieve what is beyond our vision, we must do what is in front of us. The path into the mystery is to first move through what we know today, then keep going. To walk farther than we can imagine, we must do what is in sight first.

Wherever I am standing, if I take the steps, I will get to the horizon. I don't know what is beyond that, but I will if I keep walking.

The incremental will name the distance.

Now, I am into the infinite.

...

I AM NOT THE WORDS
I SPEAK OUT LOUD,
NOT THE AIR IT TAKES TO SHAPE THEM.

I AM LIPS MAKING CROOKED CIRCLES,
THE WAY THE COSMOS MUST
WHEN IT SINGS THE INFINITE SONG,
ONE GALAXY AT A TIME.

...

Go forth, and take action
toward your infinity.

AND THEN YOU REMEMBER,
IT WAS IN YOU ALL ALONG.

Made in the USA
Columbia, SC
16 October 2025

71393360R00055